To

From

Date

Standard
BIBLE STORYBOOK SERIES

TEACHINGS OF JESUS

Retold by Carolyn Larsen

PUBLISHING

Cincinnati, Ohio

Published by Standard Publishing, Cincinnati, Ohio
www.standardpub.com
Copyright © 2012 by Standard Publishing

Printed in: China

Project editors: Elaina Meyers, Dawn A. Medill, and Marcy Levering
Cover design: Dale Meyers

Illustrations from Standard Publishing's Classic Bible Art Collection

ISBN 978-0-7847-3565-7

Library of Congress Cataloging-in-Publication Data

Larsen, Carolyn, 1950-
  Teachings of Jesus / retold by Carolyn Larsen.
     p. cm.
  ISBN 978-0-7847-3565-7 (hardcover : alk. paper)
1. Jesus Christ--Teachings--Juvenile literature. 2. Jesus Christ--
Parables--Juvenile literature. 3. Sermon on the mount--Juvenile
literature. 4. Bible stories, English--N.T. Gospels. I. Title.
  BS2416.L37 2012
  232.9'54--dc23
                                    2012002484

17 16 15 14 13 12   1 2 3 4 5 6 7 8 9

Jesus' Teachings

A very important part of Jesus' ministry was that He taught others how to know God better and how to live for Him. It was important to Jesus that people obey God and be honest about their faith in Him. Jesus taught important lessons and sometimes explained them with interesting stories. Jesus made sure that the people who needed to learn about God's love could understand His lessons. He didn't worry much about the religious leaders who already thought they knew everything.

The Sermon on the Mount *Matthew 5:1–6:4*

Large crowds of people followed Jesus everywhere He went. One day Jesus led His followers up on a mountain where He sat down with them and taught important lessons. Jesus taught His followers that God blesses people who think of others before they think

of themselves. He blesses people who are peaceful and those who take a stand for their faith in God.

Jesus taught that people who believe in God are like salt that flavors food or keeps food from spoiling. People who believe in God are like lights in dark places. Jesus said that it wouldn't be right to cover a light so that it couldn't light a room. In the same way it isn't right to hide your faith in God so that others can't see it.

Jesus also taught lessons about anger. He said that people who can't control their anger are subject to being judged by God. "So," Jesus said, "if you are angry with someone or know that someone is angry with you, go talk with them and get it settled as quickly as possible. Don't bother coming to God and asking Him for things before you take care of these anger problems."

Other lessons Jesus taught were about being pure and about keeping promises and about not seeking revenge against people who hurt you. Some people believed the old saying, "an eye for an eye" so when someone

hurt them they wanted to get even. Jesus said to leave all revenge to God.

Jesus also taught about loving your enemies. Everyone loves their friends, but only someone who has God's love in his heart can love people who hurt him. That's real love.

One important topic Jesus covered in this sermon was about taking care of the poor. It is important to help those who are needy. But Jesus said it is important to do helpful things in private, not in front of other people so that they will think good things about you.

How to Pray and Stand Strong

Matthew 6:5–7:29

A nother part of the Sermon on the Mount was when Jesus taught about prayer. He taught that prayer is a very important part of knowing God. He even gave an example of what a good prayer sounds like. That example is now called The Lord's Prayer. It teaches

us to praise God, confess our sin, and ask God for what we need.

Much of what Jesus taught about living a life of following God was how to treat other people. Jesus taught that it is important to be helpful to others, to be kind, and not to judge others. Praying for others is important too. Jesus said to keep praying, keep asking, and keep believing that God will answer. He also taught that you should treat other people the way you would like them to treat you. We call this the Golden Rule.

Some people worry a lot about what they are going to wear or what they will have to eat. Jesus said not to worry but to trust God. They can know God will take care of them because He takes care of the flowers and of all the animals. If He takes care of these things you can know He will also take care of you.

Knowing all of the things Jesus taught is important, because how a person lives shows that her faith in God is real. God is serious about who will be called His child. The pathway that leads to Heaven is clearly described by God. You can't just live

any way you want. It's important to live the way He says. If you do, your life will show kindness and concern for others.

Jesus gave an example of how important it is to believe His teachings. He said that a man who builds his house on a rock is smart because his house will stand firm in all kinds of storms. But a man who builds his house on sand will have problems when the storms come and wash the house away. Believing Jesus' teachings is like building your house on rock. You can stand strong because you are living the right way!

Jesus Talks with Nicodemus *John 3:1-21*

Late one night a man named Nicodemus came to see Jesus. Nicodemus was a Pharisee—a religious leader. He didn't want other leaders to know that he was talking with Jesus. He had important things that he wanted to discuss with Jesus. "We have all seen the miracles You do," Nicodemus said. "We know that God is with You."

Jesus said, "I want you to know that you cannot enter God's kingdom unless you are born again."

"I don't know what You mean," Nicodemus said. "Are you saying I must go back into my mother's body and be born again?"

"No, that isn't what I mean," Jesus said. "Humans can only give birth to other humans. But the Holy Spirit can give life from Heaven. That's the kind of birth I'm talking about."

"I don't understand," Nicodemus said.

"You are a Jewish religious teacher and you don't understand what I'm saying?" Jesus asked. "I am telling you that I am the Son of Man and I have come to earth so that people may have eternal life. God loved the world so much that He sent His only Son to earth so that everyone who believes in Him can be saved and have eternal life. Those who believe will not have judgment in their future. But those who do not believe will be judged. Their judgment is based on the fact that they had the light of the world right in front of them and yet they didn't believe. They hate the light because they want to live in darkness and do the sins that are part of that life. Those who want to do what is right come into the light and do what God wants."

Jesus Teaches by Telling Stories

Jesus taught people how to get along with others and how to honor God. He said that the greatest commandment from God is to love God with all your heart, soul, and mind and that the second greatest commandment is to love other people as much as you love yourself. Sometimes Jesus told stories that explained His lessons. He chose stories that people could identify with because the stories were about things the people did every day.

The Story of the Sower

Matthew 13:1-23; Mark 4:13-30; Luke 8:4-15

Jesus had a special lesson in mind when He told this story to His followers:

A farmer went out to plant some seeds. He took a handful of the seeds and began scattering them on the ground. Some of the seeds landed on a sidewalk and birds swooped down and ate up those seeds. Other seeds landed on soil that wasn't very deep and beneath that soil was a thick layer of rock. The seeds took root and plants began growing, but when the sun got hot they wilted and died. Since the soil was not very deep there wasn't enough food and water for the roots of the plants—that is why they died. Other seeds landed in the middle of a lot of weeds. Those plants tried to grow, but the weeds were stronger so they took all the food and water away from the plants. The weeds grew strong and the plants died. However, some of the seeds fell on good soil. Those seeds grew into plants that were strong and healthy. They produced a wonderful crop that was better than the farmer ever dreamed it could be.

When Jesus finished the story, His disciples came and asked Him, "Why do You always tell stories when You talk to the people?"

Jesus answered, "You have been given the gift of understanding the things of God's kingdom and you are blessed because of that. But not everyone understands. Some people will never understand because they are too stubborn. But for those who want to understand, it helps to have stories that explain the meaning."

Then Jesus explained the meaning of the story. "The seeds in this story represent the truth about God's kingdom. The sidewalk represents those who hear the truth about God's kingdom but don't understand it. The devil comes and snatches that truth away, just as the birds in the story quickly ate the farmer's seeds. The shallow soil represents those people who hear the message of God's love and accept it. But the seeds' roots don't go very deep because they don't trust God and learn more about Him. Then when they have problems they turn away from Him. The ground with lots of weeds represents people who accept God's Word and trust Him, but they try to keep other things important in their lives too. The other things choke out God's presence in their lives. The good soil is, of course, those who receive God's message, trust Him, love Him, and grow strong in Him. Their lives are good examples of God's presence in them."

The Lost Sheep *Matthew 18:12-14; Luke 15:4-7*

Another story that Jesus told was about shepherds. A lot of people who listened to Jesus teach were shepherds, so they had a special understanding of this story.

Jesus said, "Suppose a shepherd had 100 sheep in his flock. Of course, every one of those sheep is important to him. So if one sheep wanders away and is lost, the shepherd will be worried. He knows that a sheep that isn't with the rest of the flock is in danger of being attacked by a wild animal or of getting hurt. The shepherd will leave the other 99 sheep alone while he goes and looks for that one sheep. That's how important that one sheep is to him. When he finds the lost sheep he will celebrate and tell everyone who will listen how happy he is! He is probably happier about finding that one sheep than he is about the 99 sheep who didn't wander away. This story shows you how happy God is when one lost sinner comes to Him. He celebrates every person who turns away from evil to follow Him. That's because He doesn't want even one person to die without knowing Him."

The Lost Coin *Luke 15:8-10*

A fter Jesus told the story of the lost sheep, He made the same point again in another story: There was a woman who owned 10 silver coins. Her 10 coins were worth a lot of money. One day she lost one of her coins. She looked everywhere in her house for that coin. She looked in drawers and under furniture. She looked in all her pockets and everywhere she could think of. She could not find the lost coin anywhere. She lit all the lamps in her house and swept every corner of every room. The coin was no where to be found. But finally, when she had almost given up, she found the coin in the most unlikely of places! The woman was overjoyed! She danced and sang and told everyone she could find that she had found her lost coin. She called in friends and neighbors to celebrate with her because the coin that was lost was now found!

Jesus said, "Notice how happy the woman was to find her lost coin. In that same way, God rejoices over every single person who comes to Him. Even His angels celebrate when someone comes to faith in Christ!"

The Vine and the Branches *John 15:1-17*

Another time Jesus was talking with His disciples when one of them asked Him questions about why He was teaching His followers so much but not explaining things to everyone. Jesus gave them an illustration about His relationship with them. He called himself the True Vine and explained things this way: "I am the true vine and God, my Father, is the gardener. As He cares for the plants in His garden, He cuts off the branches of the plants that do not bear fruit because they are useless. Even the branches that do grow fruit have to be pruned. That means He cuts them back just a little because that keeps them healthier. You, as branches of my vine, are pruned by hearing my teachings. Stay close to me and I will stay close to you. Remember that a branch cannot grow fruit if it is cut off from the vine that provides it food and water. In the same way, you can't be fruitful if you are not connected to me. Without me you can do nothing. So, if you cut off your relationship to me, you will end up being thrown away because you are useless. Stay close to me, study my words, know me, and your prayers will be answered. My followers produce good fruit and that brings my Father joy!

"I love you all just as my Father loves me. Keep obeying my teachings just as I obey my Father. I want you to be filled with the joy of obeying and knowing my Father! Please, please, love each other. Don't let anything get in the way of that love. Real love would do anything for others; anything at all. You are truly my friends and that is why I have told you all these things. You are chosen to live in such a way that you grow fruit for my Father's kingdom. Start that by loving one another!"

A Runaway Son *Luke 15:11-32*

Jesus told another story about how happy God is and how He celebrates when people who don't know Him come to Him. The story went like this: There once was a man who had two sons. The younger son didn't like working in the fields. He went to his father and said, "I know that when you die I will get a share of your wealth. Give me my inheritance now so that I can go live on my own. I don't want to wait until you die." The father probably felt very sad about his son's decision, but he

went ahead and gave him his share of the inheritance.

The boy took the money and packed up his things and headed out. He spent the money as fast as he could. Pretty soon he had wasted all the money on wild parties and foolish things. About the same time that the boy's money ran out, a famine hit the land and it was hard to find food anywhere. The boy got very hungry but couldn't find any food. Finally the boy convinced a farmer to give him a job feeding his pigs. The boy was so hungry that even the pigs' food looked good to him! But he couldn't find any food for himself and no one would give him any.

After a while the boy realized that he had made a mistake by leaving his father's house. He thought, "Even the men who work for my father have

food to eat and here I am starving to death. I'll go home and ask my father for a job. I'll tell him that I know I don't deserve to be called his son anymore but I will beg him for a job."

So the boy started for home. He was still quite a distance from his father's house when his father saw him coming. His father had been waiting for the boy to come back home and

he was filled with love for his long-lost son. He ran to him and gave him the biggest hug ever! The young boy said, "Father, I have sinned against you. I'm not worthy of being called your son anymore."

But his father didn't pay any attention to what the boy said. He called his servants and told them, "Get busy! Bring the finest robe we have and put it on my son. Put rings on his fingers and shoes on his feet. Prepare a big feast. We are going to have a party because my son that was lost has now come home!"

In the meantime, the father's older son was out working in the fields. He didn't know that his brother had come home. But when he came back to the house at the end of the day he saw all the party preparations and smelled the wonderful dinner that had been cooked. He asked one of the servants what was happening and

was told that his brother had come home. The servant told him that his father had ordered a big party to be prepared. The older son got angry about this and went to find his father. "Why are you throwing a big party for my brother? He took your money and wasted it on foolish living. I've been here working hard for you the whole time he was in the city wasting your money. I've never once refused to do what you asked me to do. And you have never thrown a party for me; in fact, you never did anything for me. Now this boy comes home after all his foolish living and you throw him a feast? That isn't fair!"

The father was sad that his son felt this way. He said, "Look, my son. You and I are very close and I share everything with you. But we have to celebrate this day because I thought your brother was dead but now he is here! He was lost and now he is found!"

The Unforgiving Debtor *Matthew 18:21-35*

One time Peter asked Jesus a question that he had been thinking about for a while. "How often should I forgive someone who sins against me? Is seven times enough?"

"No," Jesus said. "Seventy times seven is closer to the answer! For this

very reason the kingdom of Heaven can be compared to a king who decided to collect the money owed to him by some of his servants. Things were going along well until one ser- vant came forward who owed the king millions of dollars. The servant did not have the money to pay his debt so the king ordered that the man, his wife and children, and everything the man owned be sold and the money be given to the king. The man begged the king for mercy. He promised that if the king would just be a little more patient with him he would pay the debt. The king felt sorry for the man and agreed to cancel his debt.

When that man left the king's palace he went straight to another servant who owed him a few thousand dollars. He grabbed that man by the neck and shouted, 'Pay me the money you owe me right now!' The man fell down on the ground and begged for a little more time to come up with the money. But the first man would not give him any more time. He had the man arrested and thrown in jail.

Some of the other servants saw what happened. They knew that the first man had been granted mercy from the king for his own debt. They were surprised by what he did to the man who owed him money. So the servants went to the king and told him the whole story. The king called for the man whose debt he had forgiven, "Come to see me right now!" When the man arrived the king said, "I forgave the huge debt you owed me. Then I hear that you had another man thrown in jail who owed you less than you owed me. You did this even though he begged you for mercy. Why couldn't you show him the same kindness I showed you?" Then the king had the man thrown into prison until he could pay back every penny he owed."

Then Jesus told Peter, "That is what my heavenly Father will do to you if you refuse to forgive others with your whole heart."

The Rich Young Man

Matthew 19:16-30; Mark 10:17-31; Luke 18:18-30

One time a man ran up to Jesus, knelt down on his knees, and asked this question, "Good Teacher, what do I have to do in order to know for certain that I have eternal life?"

"Why do you call me good?" Jesus answered. "Only God is truly good.

To answer your question, I remind you of the commandments: Do not murder. Do not commit adultery. Do not steal. Do not lie. Do not cheat. Honor your father and mother."

"I have kept all these commandments since the time I was very young," the man said.

Jesus felt a real love for the young man so He said, "You are only missing one thing. Sell everything that you own and give the money to the poor and you will have a great treasure in Heaven. Then come and follow me."

But the young man was very wealthy and he didn't want to sell his things. He sadly walked away from Jesus.

Jesus watched the young man leave, then He said to His disciples, "It is very hard for a rich man to get into God's kingdom." The disciples were surprised to hear Him say that. He continued, "It is easier for a camel to walk through the eye of a needle than it is for a rich man to enter Heaven."

"Well, if the rich can't be saved, then who can?" the disciples asked.

"If you depend on human strength then it is impossible. But with God all things are possible," Jesus said.

"Jesus, we have given up everything—our jobs and our families—to follow You," Peter said.

"I promise you," Jesus said, "that those who have given up everything—family, homes, and jobs—to follow me will receive a hundred times more. But they will also have to endure persecutions. But in the future they will have eternal life. Those people who think they are so important right now will be the least important in the future and the least important now will be the most important then."

A Woman Gives Everything

Mark 12:41-44; Luke 21:1-4

Jesus and His disciples went into the temple. He sat down near the box where people came to give their offerings. There were some rich people who came into the temple and put large amounts of money in the offering. They were proud of the large offerings they gave. Then a poor woman, who was a widow, came to give her offering. She dropped only two pennies in the box. But Jesus noticed her gift and He called His disciples to come to Him. He said, "That woman who just put two pennies in the box has given more than any of the rich people. They all gave a tiny part of all the money they have. But this woman gave everything she has."

The Good Samaritan *Luke 10:25-37*

A man who was an expert in religious law came to talk with Jesus one day. He asked, "What do I have to do to get eternal life?"

"What does Moses' law say?" asked Jesus.

"It says to love God with all my heart, soul, strength, and mind," the man answered. "Then it says to love my neighbor in the same way I love myself."

"Do that and you will have eternal life," Jesus said.

"Well, exactly who is my neighbor?" the man asked.

Jesus told a story to answer the man's question: There was a Jewish man who took a trip from Jericho to Jerusalem. As he was walking, robbers attacked him. They stripped his clothes off. They took his money and beat him up then left him bleeding by the side of the road. He was nearly dead.

A little while later a Jewish priest came down that same road. He saw

the poor man lying on the side of the road. But instead of helping the man, he crossed the road and hurried on his way. Later, a man who worked in the temple came along. He saw the hurt man too. But he didn't help him either. He also crossed the road and went on his way.

A Samaritan man was the next person to come down the road. Now, Jews and Samaritans don't get along with each other very well, but when the Samaritan saw the poor man lying there in a pool of blood, he felt bad for him. He washed the man's wounds and bandaged him up. Then the Samaritan picked up the man and put him on his own donkey and took him to an inn. The next day he gave the innkeeper some money and said, "I have to go on with my trip, but please take care of this man until he is well. If it costs more than this, I will pay you when I come back through this way."

"Now," Jesus said, "which of these men acted like a real neighbor?"

"The one who helped the hurt man," the religious leader said.

"Right. Now go and do the same thing," Jesus said.

The Story of the Talents

Matthew 25:14-30

J esus taught about what the kingdom of Heaven is like. He said to think of it like the man who went on a trip. Before he left town, the man gave his servants some of his own money to invest for him. He gave the first servant five bags of gold, the second servant two bags, and the third servant one bag. Then he left.

The servant who had five bags of gold invested it right away and soon had doubled his master's money. The one who had two bags got busy and doubled his money too. But the one who had one bag dug a hole in his yard and buried the money.

After a long time the master returned and called the servants to him to report on what they had done with the money. The first servant brought 10 bags of gold to his master and showed that he had doubled the money. "Good job! You have been trusted with a little responsibility and have done well; now I will give you more responsibilities. Let's celebrate!" The second servant brought four bags of gold to the master. "Good job," the master said, "you have been trusted with a little responsibility and have done well; now I will give you more responsibilities. Let's celebrate!"

Finally, the third servant brought the one bag that he had buried in the yard. "I know that you are a hard master," he said, "and I was afraid to take a chance with your money so I hid it to keep it safe."

The master wasn't happy with the third servant. "So you think I'm a hard master and that's why you hid my money? You should have at least put it in the bank so it could collect interest! Take the bag of money from this servant and give it to the man who has 10 bags of gold. Those who use well what they are given will be trusted with even more! But those who are not trustworthy will lose what they do have. Now get this useless servant out of my sight!"

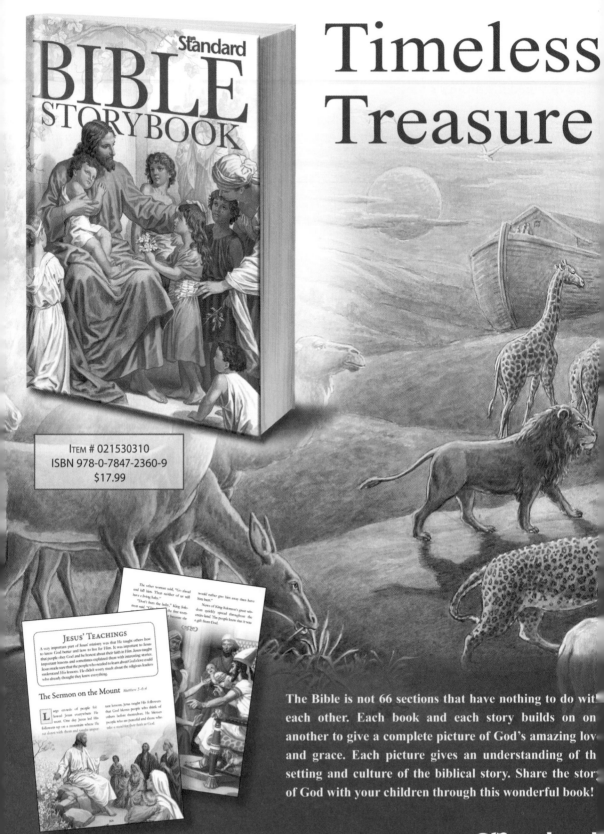